I Like Farm Animals

by
Dorothy Young

NATIONAL GEOGRAPHIC

Hampton-Brown

National Geographic and the Yellow Border are registered trademarks of the National Geographic Society.

National Geographic School Publishing
Hampton-Brown
www.NGSP.com

Printed in the USA.
RR Donnelley, Johnson City, TN

ISBN: 978-0-7362-7987-1

10 11 12 13 14 15 16 17 18 19   10 9 8 7 6 5 4 3 2

Acknowledgments and credits continue on the inside back cover.

I like the pig!

This pig is slow.

I like the horse!

This horse is fast.

I like the duck!

This duck is slow.

This duck is fast.

I like farm animals!